THE AIR INSIDE

THE AIR INSIDE

A CHILDREN'S BOOK ON HELIUM AWARENESS AND THE HIDDEN DANGERS INSIDE BALLOONS.

LoriAnn Earp

gatekeeper press
Columbus, Ohio

The Air Inside

Published by Gatekeeper Press
3971 Hoover Rd. Suite 77
Columbus, OH 43123-2839
www.GatekeeperPress.com

Copyright © 2017 by LoriAnn Earp

All rights reserved. Neither this book, nor any parts within it may be sold or reproduced in any form or by any electronic or mechanical means, including information storage and retrieval systems without permission in writing from the author. The only exception is by a reviewer, who may quote short excerpts in a review.

ISBN: 9781619847736

Printed in the United States of America

INTRODUCTION

This is a children's book about Helium balloons and being safe. In the book, we teach children about the hidden dangers of helium and that breathing air with helium is dangerous. It is not safe to make your voice sound funny. Things you can't see can hurt you. With this book I hope to change how we view helium and how to be safe with it.

DEDICATION

This book is dedicated in memory of Ashley Jean Long and Jordan McDowell. These girls lost their lives to helium while trying to make their voices sound funny. With this book I hope to save lives and change how the world views Helium. Helium is dangerous in any form.....

Have you ever wondered about what's inside of a balloon? What makes the balloon float in the air?

Or what happens when you breathe in the air inside?

Balloons are bright and exciting but there are hidden dangers inside.

Helium is what is used to make balloons float. This is a type of invisible gas that is dangerous. To fill the balloons with helium, a tank is needed.

Some people have found that breathing in helium makes their voices change. It sounds funny. But this is a very bad idea.

The air inside "the helium" is dangerous.

It can hurt you badly if you breathe it. Balloons seem harmless but they can hurt you.

Never breathe the air from inside a balloon. It is unsafe. Never breathe the air inside the tanks used to fill balloons. This keeps you safe from the danger.

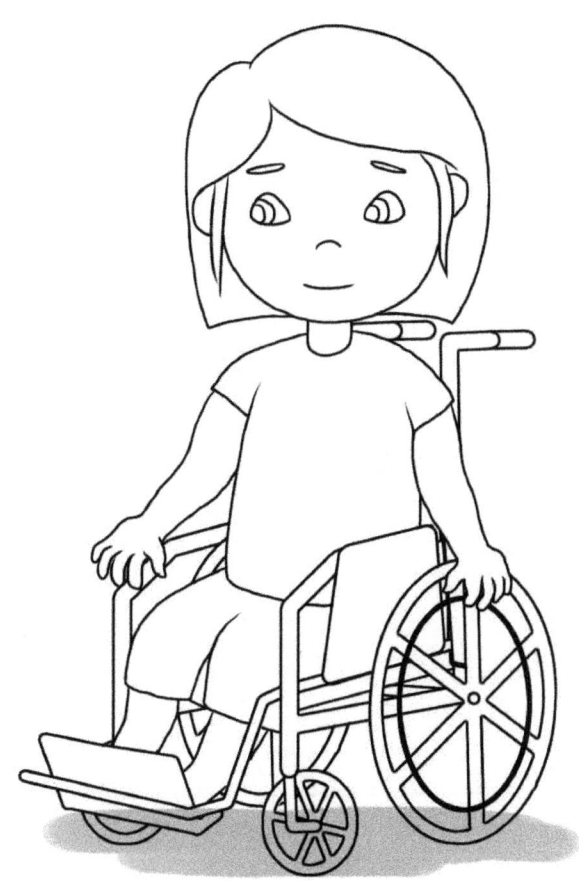

Trying to change your voice too sound funny is dangerous. Never! Ever! Ever! breathe the air inside a balloon or a helium tank used to fill floating balloons.

Interactive questions

1. **WHAT IS HELIUM?**
   It is an invisible gas used to make balloons float.

2. **WHAT DOES INVISIBLE MEAN?**
   It means something that you cannot see.

3. **WHAT PARTS OF YOUR BODY CAN HELIUM HURT?**
   It can hurt your lungs, your heart, and your brain.

4. **HOW CAN YOU STAY SAFE WITH YOUR HELIUM BALLOON?**
   By not breathing in the helium.

Match the dots

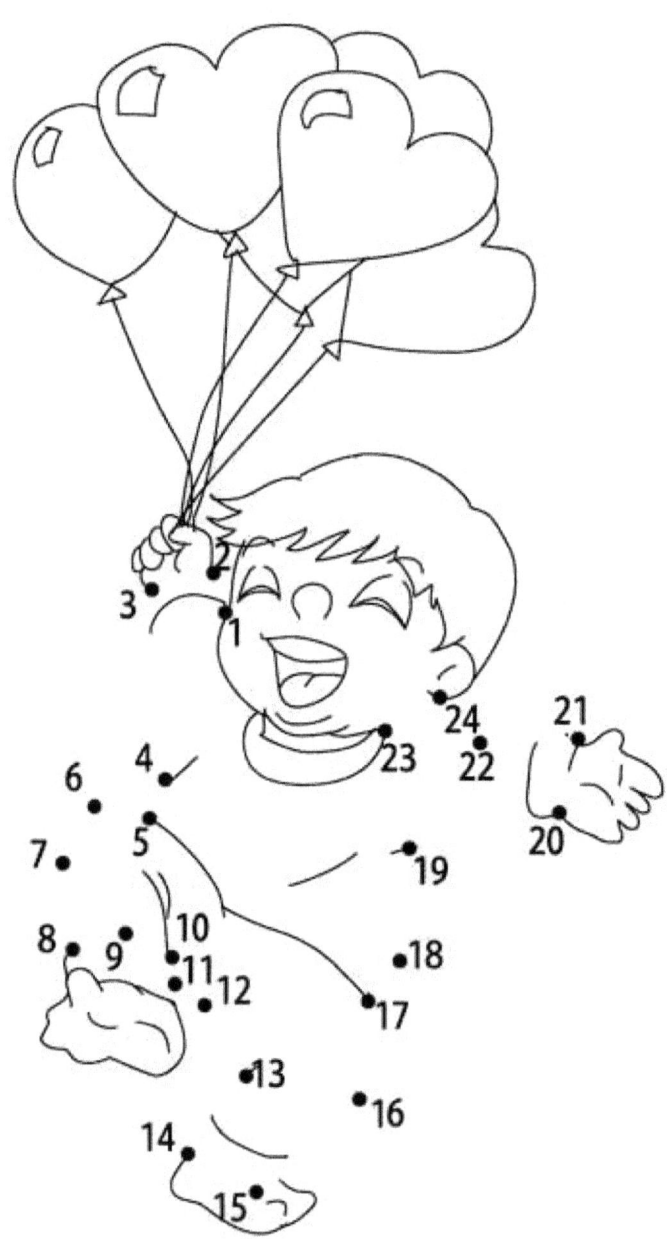

How many ways can you find to reach the balloon?

Color Me!

Color Me!

Word Search
Can you find them?

K	I	H	M	C	F	K	A	M	E	D	N
F	S	S	S	M	D	E	N	T	I	S	I
T	Q	U	D	F	R	F	S	O	Q	G	N
A	M	R	I	A	L	A	Y	S	C	J	V
N	D	B	A	L	L	O	O	N	W	Z	I
K	Q	H	D	H	E	I	A	P	H	T	S
S	A	F	E	G	L	N	B	T	H	E	I
T	U	O	F	B	R	E	A	T	H	E	B
C	O	O	C	I	K	G	B	A	Y	T	L
T	B	T	A	S	U	R	B	C	L	H	E

WORD LIST

BALLOON   AIR
TANK   FLOAT
INVISIBLE   SAFE
BREATHE

WHAT PARTS OF YOUR BODY CAN HELIUM HURT IF INHALED?

Lungs,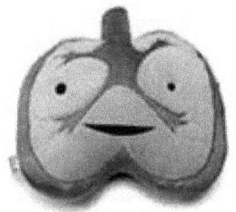

heart,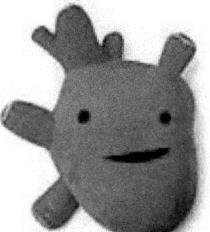

and our brain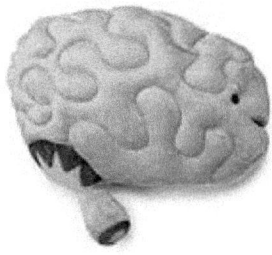

Can you draw yourself being safe with helium?

www.ingramcontent.com/pod-product-compliance
Lightning Source LLC
LaVergne TN
LVHW072053060526
838200LV00061B/4729